Oceans of the World

Pacific Ocean

Louise and Richard Spilsbury

heinemann
raintree

© 2015 Heinemann Raintree
an imprint of Capstone Global Library, LLC
Chicago, Illinois

To contact Capstone Global Library please
call 800-747-4992, or visit our web site
www.capstonepub.com

Edited by Penny West
Designed by Steve Mead
Original illustrations © Capstone Global Library Ltd 2015
Picture research by Tracy Cummins
Production by Victoria Fitzgerald
Originated by Capstone Global Library Ltd

Library of Congress Cataloging-in-Publication Data
Spilsbury, Louise.
   Pacific Ocean / Louise Spilsbury and Richard Spilsbury.
       pages cm.—(Oceans of the world)
   Includes bibliographical references and index.
   ISBN 978-1-4846-0771-8 (hb)—ISBN 978-1-4846-0777-0 (pb)—ISBN 978-1-4846-0789-3 (ebook) 1. Oceanography—
Pacific Ocean—Juvenile literature. 2. Pacific Ocean—Juvenile literature. I. Spilsbury, Richard, 1963- II. Title.

   GC771.S65 2015
   910.9164—dc23   2014010885

This book has been officially leveled by using the F&P Text Level Gradient™ Leveling System.

Acknowledgments
We would like to thank the following for permission to reproduce photographs: Getty Images: AFP PHOTO/Robyn Beck, 19,
David Wall Photo, 15 Top, Mauricio Handler, 25, Nick Hall, 18, SADATSUGU TOMIZAWA/AFP, 11; Newscom: Jonathan
Alcorn/ZUMAPRESS.com, 27 Top; Shutterstock: Anton Balazh, 7, Carolina K. Smith MD, 4, cdrin, 20 Bottom, chungking, 21
Bottom, Dhoxax, 16 Bottom, DmitrySerbin, 14, EpicStockMedia, Cover Top, Fiona Ayerst, 17, Igor Plotnikov, 23, leoks, 12,
leonello calvetti, Cover Middle, Naaman Abreu, 22, Tanya Puntti, Cover Bottom, Vlad61, 26 Bottom, Vladislav Gurfinkel, 13,
worldswildlifewonders, 24, Zmiter, Design Element.

We would like to thank Michael Bright for his invaluable help in the preparation of this book.

READ MORE

Hawbaker, Emily. *Energy Lab for Kids: 40 Exciting Experiments to Explore, Create, Harness, and Unleash Energy.* Beverly, MA: Quarry, 2017.

O'Donnell, Liam. *The Shocking World of Electricity with Max Axiom Super Scientist: 4D An Augmented Reading Science Experience.* Graphic Science 4D. North Mankato, MN.: Capstone Press, 2019.

Roby, Cynthia. *Discovering STEM at the Amusement Park.* STEM in the Real World. New York: PowerKids Press, 2016.

CRITICAL THINKING QUESTIONS

1. What is the difference between potential and kinetic energy?

2. Read pages 6–9. What type of energy would electricity change to once it powers a motor to make a machine move?

3. Sound moves in waves from a source. Why do you think sounds are quieter the farther you are from their source? Why are they louder when you are closer to the source?

INTERNET SITES

Energy in a Roller-Coaster Ride
https://www.pbslearningmedia.org/resource/hew06.sci.phys.maf.rollercoaster/energy-in-a-roller-coaster-ride/

How Do Roller Coasters Work?
https://wonderopolis.org/wonder/how-do-roller-coasters-work

Types of Energy
https://www.solarschools.net/knowledge-bank/energy/types

INDEX

Contents

Some words are shown in bold, **like this**. You can find out what they mean by looking in the glossary.

About the Pacific Ocean

The Pacific is one of the world's five oceans. An ocean is a huge area of salty water. The Pacific is the biggest ocean on Earth. It covers about a third of the surface of our planet.

The Pacific Ocean covers more of the surface of Earth than all the dry land put together!

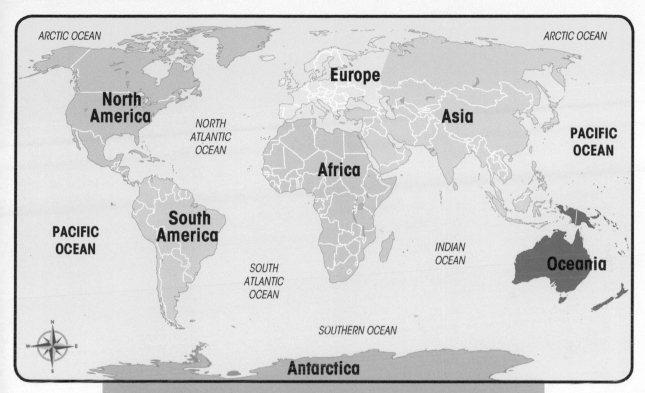

Europe

North
America

NORTH
ATLANTIC
OCEAN

Asia

PACIFIC
OCEAN

Africa

PACIFIC
OCEAN

South
America

INDIAN
OCEAN

Oceania

SOUTH
ATLANTIC
OCEAN

SOUTHERN OCEAN

Antarctica

The Pacific Ocean is joined to the other oceans of the world and water flows between them.

The Pacific Ocean stretches from the Arctic Ocean in the north to the Southern Ocean in the south. To the east of the Pacific Ocean lie the **continents** of North America and South America. To the west lie the continents of Asia and Oceania.

An ocean is mostly open water. **Seas** are smaller areas of an ocean found near the land. A sea is also usually partly surrounded by land. The South China Sea, Philippine Sea, Sulu Sea, and Celebes Sea are all part of the Pacific Ocean.

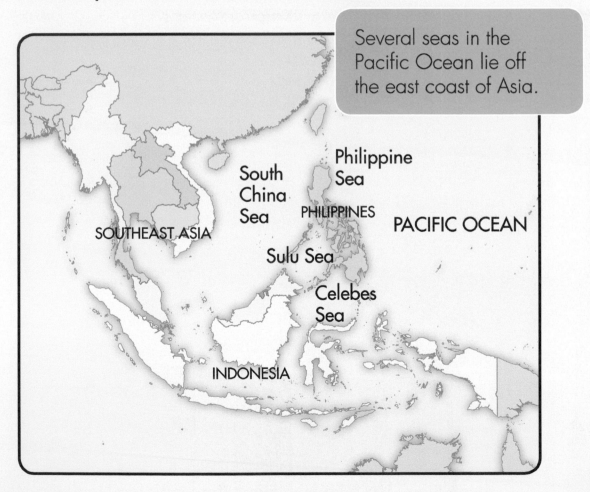

Several seas in the Pacific Ocean lie off the east coast of Asia.

Philippine Sea

South China Sea

PHILIPPINES

PACIFIC OCEAN

SOUTHEAST ASIA

Sulu Sea

Celebes Sea

INDONESIA

Arctic Ocean

Ships travel through the Bering Strait from the Pacific Ocean to the Arctic Ocean.

Bering Strait

Bering Sea

Pacific Ocean

The Bering Sea is a sea at the far north of the Pacific Ocean. At the top of this sea is the Bering Strait. A **strait** is a narrow corridor of water that links a sea to an ocean.

Geography

The bottom of the ocean has different features, just like the land we live on. In the center of the Pacific, the ocean floor is fairly flat. In some places, there are underwater mountains with steep sides and flat tops. These are called seamounts.

Pacific Ocean fact file

Surface area (excluding adjacent seas):	63,800,000 square miles (165,250,000 square kilometers)
Average depth:	13,123 feet (about 4,000 meters)
Deepest point:	The Mariana Trench 35,840 feet (10,924 meters) below sea level
Size of the Mariana Trench:	1,580 miles (2,540 kilometers) long and 43 miles (69 kilometers) at the widest point

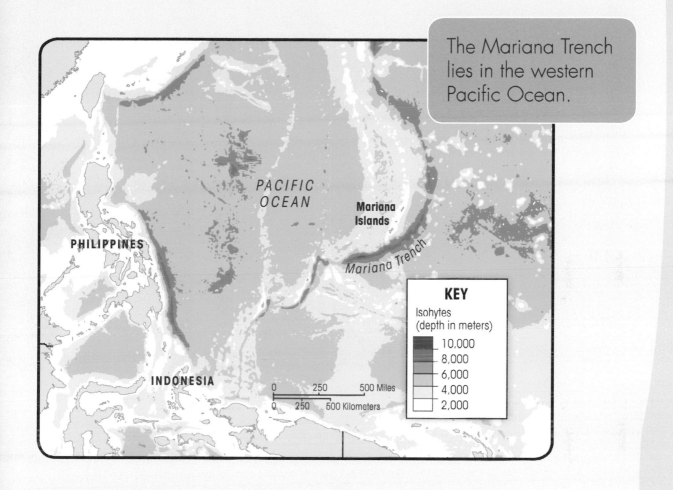

The Mariana Trench lies in the western Pacific Ocean.

PACIFIC OCEAN

Mariana Islands

Mariana Trench

PHILIPPINES

INDONESIA

KEY

Isohytes
(depth in meters)

10,000
8,000
6,000
4,000
2,000

0   250   500 Miles
0 250   500 Kilometers

There are also deep trenches in the Pacific. A trench is a very long, deep, narrow ditch. The biggest Pacific trench is the Mariana Trench. The Challenger Deep in the Marianna Trench is the deepest point on Earth!

The edge of the Pacific Ocean is known as the Ring of Fire because most **volcanoes** are created here. Earth's surface is split into pieces called **plates**. Beneath the Pacific Ocean is the Pacific plate. Volcanoes happen when hot liquid rock from inside Earth rises up in the gap where plates meet.

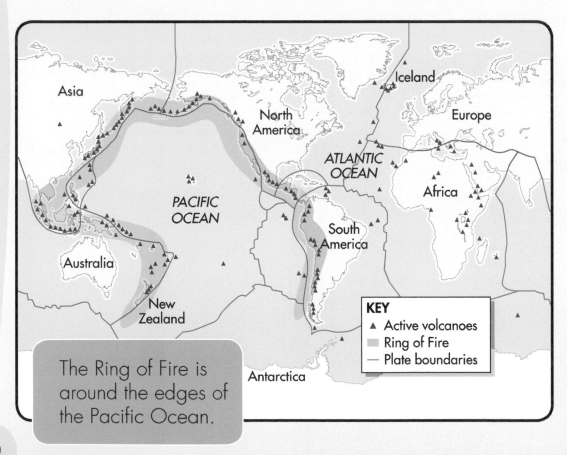

The Ring of Fire is around the edges of the Pacific Ocean.

KEY
▲ Active volcanoes
▇ Ring of Fire
— Plate boundaries

Giant tsunami waves can crash onto land and cause terrible damage and destruction.

Most of the world's **earthquakes** happen in the Ring of Fire, too. When the Pacific plate scrapes against another plate, the ground shakes and causes an earthquake. When there is an earthquake under the **sea**, this can cause a giant wave called a tsunami.

Temperature

The Pacific Ocean is so big that its water has different temperatures. Near the **Poles** it is very cold, so the water is freezing and can turn to ice. Near the **Equator**, the water in the Pacific Ocean is warmer.

Many tourists visit beaches around the Equator where the waters of the Pacific Ocean are very warm.

This is a satellite picture
of a huge hurricane over
the Pacific Ocean.

Typhoons or hurricanes sometimes form over
the Pacific Ocean. These are huge, whirling
winds that happen when warm ocean water
heats the air above it. The warm air rises, and
this causes winds. When hot air rises quickly,
the winds spin very quickly, too.

Islands

There are 25,000 islands in the Pacific, which is more than in any other ocean! An island is an area of land surrounded by water. New Zealand is a country made up of two large islands and many smaller islands in the southwestern Pacific Ocean.

This lovely beach is on North Island, one of New Zealand's two main islands.

The Fijian archipelago is in the South Pacific Ocean.

The country of Fiji is made up of an **archipelago** of different islands. An archipelago is a group or row of islands close together. There are more than 800 islands in Fiji, including over 500 small islands called islets.

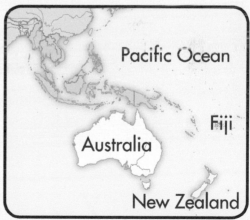

Pacific Ocean

Australia

Fiji

New Zealand

Some Pacific islands are old **volcanoes**. When a volcano **erupts** underwater, the hot, liquid rock cools down quickly and becomes solid rock. The top of this volcanic rock can poke above the water to form an island!

Hawaii

Pacific Ocean

Australia

New Zealand

This island in Hawaii formed from a volcano.

This colorful coral reef is off the coast of the Raja Ampat islands, in Indonesia.

Some volcanic islands in the Pacific Ocean are surrounded by **coral reefs**. Coral is made by millions of tiny animals called polyps. Each polyp builds a skeleton of **limestone** around itself. A coral reef is made of millions of these limestone cases.

Resources

There are lots of useful resources in the Pacific Ocean. People catch more fish here than in any other ocean. In the cold waters of the North Pacific Ocean, big boats called trawlers catch fish such as salmon, tuna, and herring.

Many trawlers have freezers on board to store the caught fish.

People drill for oil under the ocean floor from platforms like these.

People drill under the floor of the Pacific Ocean to get oil and gas. We use these fuels for energy to power vehicles and other machines. People take sand and gravel from the ocean floor for building. They also dig up copper and other metals to make things such as cell phones.

Ports

Lots of ships carry goods and people across the Pacific Ocean. Seattle, Washington, is a city with a big **port** on the west coast of North America. A port is a place where ships load and unload.

Seattle

North America

People can get on a cruise ship in Seattle and travel to Alaska and Canada.

Ships take things made in China across the Pacific to sell all over the world.

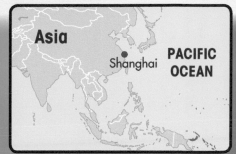

Asia

Shanghai

PACIFIC OCEAN

The port at Shanghai is very busy. Shanghai is a city on the east coast of China. Cranes load containers full of computers, toys, and other goods onto ships.

People

Many people work on the coasts around the Pacific Ocean. In Mexico, there are huge hotels where tourists come to visit the beaches. Many people work here in the hotels, restaurants, and stores.

Some workers take tourists out on boats or on other trips.

Fishing families live in these stilt houses on beaches in the Philippines.

Some people in Washington state live in houseboats on the Pacific Ocean. In the Philippines, some families live in houses on wooden legs called stilts. This keeps the houses dry when the **tide** comes in.

Animals

There are many different animals in the Pacific Ocean. Sea otters live near the coast. They dive to catch clams, crabs, and other small animals underwater. They eat lying on their backs on the water's surface.

Sea otters wrap themselves in seaweed so they don't float away while they sleep!

The giant Pacific octopus can be as big as 30 feet (9 meters) across, when spread out across the ground!

The giant Pacific octopus is the biggest octopus in the world. These amazing animals catch fish, shrimp, and other animals with their long arms. They can change color to hide against rocks on the floor of the Pacific Ocean.

Famous Places

One of the most famous places in the Pacific Ocean is the Great Barrier Reef. This is the biggest **coral reef** in the world. It runs more than 1,250 miles (2,000 kilometers) along the northeast coast of Australia. It contains many beautiful, different-colored corals.

Great Barrier Reef

Australia

Sea turtles, dolphins, and many other amazing animals live on the Great Barrier Reef.

This plastic waste from the Great Pacific Garbage Patch washed up on a beach in Hawaii.

United States

Mexico

Great Pacific
Garbage Patch

The Great Pacific Garbage Patch is not beautiful. It is an enormous area of plastic waste floating in the Pacific Ocean. It has been called the biggest garbage dump in the world. Some of the waste is too small to see, but all of it is bad for the ocean and the animals in it.

Fun Facts

- The Great Barrier Reef is the only living thing on Earth that astronauts can see from space.

- Over 65 percent of the world's fish caught from the oceans comes from the Pacific Ocean.

- The word "pacific" means "peaceful." The explorer Magellan gave the Pacific Ocean its name because the waters were calm when he first discovered it in 1521.

- If Mount Everest were put into the deepest part of the Mariana Trench, then its top would still be 1.4 miles (2 kilometers) underwater.

- The center of the Pacific Ocean is 1,670 miles (2,688 kilometers) from the nearest land, making it the most remote point on Earth!

Quiz

1 Which is the biggest ocean on Earth?

2 Which is the deepest **trench** on Earth?

3 Why is the area around the Pacific Ocean called the Ring of Fire?

4 Where is the world's biggest garbage dump?

4 The Great Pacific Garbage Patch in the Pacific Ocean is the world's biggest garbage dump.

3 The Ring of Fire is where lots of **volcanoes** happen.

2 The Mariana Trench is the deepest trench on Earth.

1 The Pacific Ocean is the biggest ocean on Earth.

Answers

Glossary

archipelago group or row of islands close together

continent one of seven huge areas of land on Earth

coral reef long line of stony coral rock near the surface of the ocean

earthquake sudden and violent shaking of the ground

erupt when a volcano explodes and hot, melted rock called lava and dust spurt out of it

Equator imaginary line around the middle of Earth

limestone type of hard rock or stone

plate giant piece of rock that floats on the hot rock in the center of Earth

Poles the two points at opposite ends of Earth, the North Pole and South Pole

port place at the edge of an ocean where ships stop

sea smaller area of an ocean usually found near the land and usually partly surrounded by land

strait narrow corridor of water that links seas and oceans

tide way the sea moves up and down the shore twice a day

volcano hole in Earth from which fiery hot, melted rock called lava spurts out

Find Out More

Books

Labrecque, Ellen. *Deep Oceans* (Earth's Last Frontiers). Chicago: Heinemann Library, 2014.

MacQuitty, Miranda. *Ocean* (DK Eyewitness). New York: Dorling Kindersley, 2013.

Newland, Sonya. *Ocean Animals* (Saving Wildlife). Mankato, Minn.: Smart Apple Media, 2012.

Web sites

Facthound offers a safe, fun way to find Internet sites related to this book. All of the sites on Facthound have been researched by our staff.

Here's all you do:
Visit www.facthound.com
Type in this code: 9781484607718

Index